Poems from the Lawnchair

by

Vickie V. Adams

Inspirations from 21st Century Life

Vickie Vaughn Adams

Copyright © 2011 Vickie V. Adams

All rights reserved.

ISBN: 1463584512
ISBN-13: 9781463584511

LCCN:

DEDICATION

This book is dedicated to my Lord Jesus who gave me the ideas, inspiration and drive to complete this project. My mother Linnie Mae, Adam Jacob, Azure Elizabeth, Devon, Dylan, Leviticus (*los tres*), Kristina, Jordan, Autumn and Darien. These are the trees and the roots. I would also like to thank the Uncles who have been there for us over the years. They have been such a blessing and there in our time of need. A shout out to my graduate classmates who have been so encouraging!

Con mucho felicidades y amor siempre, mi familia!

"Sweet V."

37	My Favorite Chore
38	Dreamers
39	Advice for Bullies
40	Look at Those Genes!
41	Perfect Combination
42	The Producers

ACKNOWLEDGMENTS

This book of songs from the heart is dedicated to my Lord Jesus who gave me the ideas and inspiration. My mother Linnie Mae, Adam Jacob, Azure Elizabeth, Devon, Dylan, and Leviticus, Kristina LeAnn, Jordan Elizabeth, Autumn Marie (Bear), Darian Deonte (Bubby). The aforementioned people are the roots and the fruit of my tree limb. Also cheers to great and supportive uncles Uncle Buddy and Uncle Jimmy, Millicent Noel, Ruth, Louis, Curtis, Clara, and a shout out to my graduate classmates who also encouraged me greatly this past year.

Con mucho felicidades y amor siempre mi familia!

Sweet V.

1 - CREATURE FEATURES

Media Model

Computer in the library, at my house resting on the desk.

No one said it would make life more exciting or even make it less.

Mini *televison* playing and laying upon my bed

Propped up for full view, not the book that **should** be read.

Cellphones causing cancer, rumored so they say.

Children asked at night to stash those vivid images away.

Microwaves from the oven and *radiowaves* vibe through air

Silent pollution radiates from Earth, at *computer*s millions sit and stare.

Texting to an audience or blogging to far away strangers.

Predators veiled in darkness, too many hidden dangers.

Comments to fellow teachers resting in the lounge,

"*How'd we ever make it before all these things got found?*"

Zerox copier, the first it used to be.

Now replaced by computer screens, with invisible LEDs.

Mimeo-*mimeograph*, I loved the smell of ink.

Rotate the chambered cylinder faster, today they're now extinct.

Satellites beam directions from blinking distant stars,

So we can study Venus or maybe rust-red glowing Mars.

No more privacy, the monster search engines spy.

What are your valued numbers and how much did you buy?

People hawking friendships and playing juvey media games.

Sometimes I often wish that life was more mundane.

Invisible noise radiates, becomes a constant friend,

Even when it's silenced the ruckus never ends.

The stream still leaks into your psyche, so much peace is lost.

At what expense will you sacrifice, have you really weighed the cost?

Once we were warned of the dangers that robots will take what humans need.

They need no fifteen - minute breaks due to their fatigue.

Reality has hit as computers take control of mortals reigns

Humans are becoming extinct, and soon might be contained.

Vickie Vaughn Adams

Hope

Hope has built mighty nations and crushed the tender heart.

It's saved families and also ripped some apart.

Hope is like a double-edged sword. It holds two parts together or steals long awaited reward.

What is hope for you? I'll tell you what it can be—

A life-saving raft on a dark raging sea.

Hope is the foundation of religions and dreams that top the spires.

Hope shores up the depths of our deepest, longed for desires.

Hope has given life to battered broken limbs.

It's also seen the demise of chances oh so very slim.

Dreams of riches and games of chance.

The realization that an invalid might dance.

Desires to one day be, the belle of the ball.

Marry a prince and end up with it all.

Hope has given life to broken bodes in their beds, limbs crushed, bodies withered they still "*hope*" on ahead.

Surely love will come to fill an empty soul.

A hand to hold as time marches on, both together as we grow weak and old.

Hope is inspiration or an enemy of precious time.

What is hope in your life?

This only you can truly define.

Vickie Vaughn Adams

SPIDER

The spider sits and spends its sticky bed.

It's threads are lies that fall like dew, untruths a silver tongue has said.

The lines are all symmetrical, spun from deep and sweetest dreams.

When you get trapped, you find they weren't what they once had seemed.

As you slowly move towards your painful death—hope blinds you cannot see.

Webs woven of steel, lithe and strong—now you can't seem to break free.

You stepped into those lies, spun of gossamer threads,

Following your heart, not heeding those signs of dread.

In too far, quite late to turn around.

After spider's finished, only empty shells are found.

He pricks you with his poison and takes away your strength.

He cares for nothing but his dangerous intent.

You lie there, innards liquefied and fright takes a strangle hold.

Your precious body and strength seep out given over like glistening gold

All you sought was a strong heart to care, and based upon desires, you've

been caught in his evil lair.

Had you listened to the warning in your head,

you'd have had a full life and would not his empty soul have fed.

Beware the spider, with venom in his kiss.

Heed wisdom when seeking love or your end will be like this.

Vickie Vaughn Adams

A FRIGHTFUL BEAST

This beast called anger, rages within my chest.

Begging to be free, it will not let me rest.

The strides that I make to take me to the top, it topples opportunities like a child's toy building blocks.

An errant word, meant to cause me hurt--Causes the beast, itself to assert.

Wisdom cries out, *"Halt before it's too, too late!"* All the plans you've made, derailed by monstrous hate.

The beast knows no reason, when it's ire is risen. It screams to be free of it's "reasoning' prison.

"What did you say? You trying to make me look weak?" I'll show you, if it's strength that you seek!"

You try to push it down, 'cause you know the damage it will do. The rage inside hurts me, although directed toward you.

I try to hold it in. I struggle to push it down. But it claws its way up and out of my throat, it's bound!

"*Let me out!*" "*Set me free!*" I'll set all their wrongs to right. But I know within myself that these are lies. I never win these fights.

"*Help me, Help me!*" I don't want to be like this. A victim of emotions, a prisoner of these fits.

It's so strange, how this rage takes over and wins. It only abates, when it's ignited and then when it ends.

The bible says that, "*Anger rests in the bosom of a fool.*" It uses and abuses me. I'm left, looking like a tool.

Many accolades and relations I have thrown away, because I can't stay this beast, and keep it 's will at bay.

I've lost jobs, hurt friends and close ones to my heart. Too late the damage is done and "*sorry*" too small a remark!

The beast is satisfied, enjoying the meal that it has won. It snarls and roars with pride.

The beast relieved the pressure that felt like tons inside.

I don't want this animal, living within me,

 "Take it all away, it's not who I want to be."

The wise man knows that this poison, must be bled out of the heart.

Clip the claws and teeth of the beast or your life <u>will</u> be shorn apart.

2 - MODERN LIFE

Fifteen Minutes

Fire in the belly, burns and simmers slow

Push it down, cover it up, but the raging fire's aglow.

So hungry for fame, people try anything,

Peeling off their clothes or dodging arrows and slings.

Highlights of the sick, fear of germs and lovers of junk

Hoarding trash in closets, under beds and in trunks.

Drugging and boozing, excessively rude –

latent desires too lascivious and lewd.

Too thin or so shapely, balances cans on a rear

Kittens, dogs and cats endearing and queer.

Vickie Vaughn Adams

Wealth to excess, cheating partners engaged in exchange

Serial killers, no right to be seen deluded and deranged.

Sinking in the muck of reality T.V. shows,

Minds numbed, eyes glazed by their villainous blows.

Compete to lose fat, makeovers and glam.

Chopshops, tattoos, plastic surgery exams.

Venting dirty laundry all day and all night.

Maury's "baby-moma's" and Springer's girl fights.

Americans on fire for their fifteen minutes of fame.

Little do they know, that *their glory is their shame*.

RESIDUE

Residue a scent or resonance left behind

An odorous fragrance of feelings so gentle and kind.

New places and odd scenes how will you respond?

React positively to reinforce loosened bonds.

Imprint on the lives of passing strangers,

Calm and collected, no remnant of eminent danger.

Trials and tests daily will surely come to pass

Will you elevate someone or somehow that aim surpass?

Surrounded by toxic attitudes and behavior on water, land and air.

A gentle reply to an evil report, can extinguish hardened residue that might flare.

The remnants of your beauteous aura and spirit resonate,

vibrations from your gentle soul and into God's universe will not abate.

What kind of residue do you leave throughout your day?

Is it shimmering in the light as you help a lost one find the way?

Is it paled by impatience towards the person waiting in line?

Is this the residue of your precious life unrefined?

Is your residual past so bright it outshines starry nights?

Is it the love for your fellow man that makes your heart so light?

Love isn't what you say it's really how you live.

Are you afraid to love and freely share what love can easily give?

All that remains, is what we leave behind.

I want my legacy so bright, the sun pales in comparison to it's beautiful shine.

A True Friend

Animal companions were found in Eden's garden.

Comforted fallen man, whose heart through sin was hardened.

It is said that a true friend *"loveth at all times."*

The same can be said of the loyal companion canine.

We shed our outer skins giving off our scents.

They shed their fur as though it were a warm sweater made of seasonal lint.

Odors dissipate from both mammals into the air,

but canine snouts record them all and remain with them everywhere.

Hyperactive kids, the pets fetch and run.

Aversions to water, but not to kids and fun.

Strong personalities need to learn the rules,

Life is their training field and not obedience school.

Many a canine friend has saved a valued friend's life.

Companions for the lonely, a balm that soothes the strife.

Searching for cadavers, herding in the cattle—

Seeking out the mines and leading charge in the battle.

Barking at errant strangers, that wander into their sphere.

Sitting at their master's feet, a family member dear.

Wake a sleeping family, when raging fires consume the house,

Chasing at its tail, like it's a tiny country mouse.

With little reason to go on, my friend I want a pet!

An important part of family life, a friend with wet nose, don't you ever forget.

In the family photos, in every single frame –

love unconditional has a simple name.

Ruff, ruff!

The Liar

I met a liar on my travels when doing my tasks one day,

I didn't want to be bothered, but he claimed he had something very important to say!

The liar said to me, "Miss, *might I walk with you*?"

The skeptic in me relied, "*I guess, what harm could this one do*?"

He claimed to have stalked huge bears, with curved and sharpened claws.

He said he WAS a major player, who skirted the sanctioned laws.

He was a banker *and* then a plumber *and* then a sailor of the seas.

I kept pondering what does this liar want, why is he bothering me?

I was reticent of giving him my precious and reluctant ear,

but his words became sad and tender, as he seemed extremely sincere.

I was aware that he was a liar, but couldn't pry my ears from his tales.

His "big fish" stories and million dollar sales.

We continued to walk and I feigned interest in it all.

Especially when he came to the tale of his great and tragic fall.

He began, "*I once had a mansion and a fine family.*

I had a wife and a kid – it was then just us three".

I wanted more than **my** finances could afford,

so I did evil things to attain a greater recompense and reward.

I set up a friend to take the fall for a terrible crime.

Now he's up a creek, in prison and doing some very hard time.

The lie that I told, was to extort my truest and dearest friend.

He was unable to repay his debt --- and not so well hidden sin.

I repented of my lies, when I saw how they destroyed his once goodly life.

He lost his family, his home and his extremely devoted wife.

When my beloved wife discovered the source of my ill-gotten gains,

She would not forgive me, because of the deepest of pain.

She left me and took my child, along with our family home.

One can't really live fully, when experiencing life deserted and alone.

I decided right then, that there'll be no more lies , can you see?

I'll wait right here, while you change this three-dollar bill at the store (over there) for me?

3 – YOU'VE GOT ISSUES

Night Lights & Frights

What do you see from the corner of your eye?

A dark, shadow from the periphery I spy.

While laying low on my bed,

"*Did you see something*?" to my Fuzzy Brown Bear I said.

The streetlight streams through the seams in the blinds.

What is it? *Que pasa*? Am I losing my mind?

Laughing at my own doubts and fear.

What is that creaking in the hallway I hear?

Laying on the bed and staring at the walls.

Is that a spider or the web on which it crawls.

Peering down the hall in the darkness of the night.

Was that a whispy white veil, that trailed out of my sight.

No need to leave a lamp on in the halls.

Make excuses to yourself, "*I need it, I might fall!*"

Brown Bear just lies there staring straight into the air.

He has no fears or claws to strike

at the invisible nightmare.

Alone in the house, no one is aware of the

silly mindgames darkness plays

when light is not there.

The shadows play games, into corners

and minds they dart. Creeping up halls

and stairways—terrorizing feeble hearts.

 # Shacking Up

Shows fear of commitment.

Holding out for a better deal?

Actually you're not enough!

Clause for escape

Killing time

Instead of?

Next in line!

Go back to square one.

Unless I have it my way ….

Please *let me* introduce the next act.

Poems from the Lawnchair – Volume I

Phobic – Part I

Problems controlling fear

Horror of the unreal

Out of control

Behavioral issues

Intelligent people understand but can't …

Control these fears.

 # Phobias – Part I I

My loved ones are hurt and become very sad,

When I take out my alcohol and gauze scrubbing pad.

My son has asked me, "Ma, *do you think that we're unclean?"*

I can't explain to him, *"Son I'm really not trying to be mean!"*

Truly, I'm not sure what's at the root of all this fear.

It just came upon me one day, and for what reason, I'm not clear.

I go to the library and sponge off the mouse.

I also wash my hands a thousand times in my house.

When making my food, I feel as if for surgery I prepare.

I can't let one invisible germ into my air.

Too much work, but fear is in control!

Why must I let it continue to take this toll?

I stand in the restaurant front, and preen to view the grill,

If they lay down the utensils, I don't really want the meal.

I go through the house and wipe down all light switches.

If I make a small snack, it requires rewashing clean dishes.

I feel all wrong, if I don't have my bleach.

Even the kids at school, pick up what I'm trying to teach.

I tell myself **every single day**, "*You can't enjoy your life and continue on this way.*"

I've pinpointed several reasons for my manic phobic ways.

I'll explain the first thought planted long ago many days.

My sister the nurse, once sincerely told me,

You'll get creeped out, if the germs under the microscope you could really see.

Once I got sick, when I went out on a date.

I know it was the unclean food and drink that I **should not have** ate.

I think the major reason for all of this worry and whine,

is that I desire to control what really isn't mine.

The Boat

I was once svelte and slim, with a figure just like you.

Then time and age took their toll around age *thirty-two*.

Sugar, cookies, icecream, donuts and cake.

In the middle of the night *with worries*, I snuck downstairs and ate.

Had a few kids and that took all my strength,

I look back in time and wonder where it all went.

I want to be young and slim again, but that boat has sailed.

I look at the puffy muffin top and in agony I wail.

Who is this person with fat rolls and lines?

Pictures plastered all over the house, remind me that time hasn't been kind.

That's it, I'm going, off to the gym!

I get sidetracked and dawdle, "*That sure won't get me trim!*"

I stiffen my resolve, rise up early and say ....

"*I will, I will make my run for fitness today!*"

Put on my sneakers, from room to room I stride.

Next thing I know, it's totally dark outside!

Who is this person resigned to "*fat-fate*".

Bemoaning that she'll never again get a date?

Look at models and former "*blubber lovers*" like me.

If they can do it, I too can be "fat-free"!

I can admit to these things, 'cause I lack resolve.

I have lots of solutions, but this problem evolves.

Will I ever make it to this shore and emerge a new me?

Or shall I drag on , with this fat making spree?

Only time will tell if my ship has truly sailed.

It seems I'll only win the lard war, if they put me in jail.

ADD Time

Time and patience, the only way to go.

Life is a game of waiting, if life you've lived you'll know.

I have a hard way, giving my attention.

It's *not* cause you don't matter, I won't fail to mention.

Sitting in the traffic or waiting in the car.

I can't help but feel like a kid, *and hope it's not too far*.

Hurry! Please hurry! I cannot seem to wait.

"*Will you please make me a two second sh*ake?"

"I'm *hungry, I want my burger now*".

McDonalized society, "*For goodness sake, please don't have a cow!*"

Pull a tiny ticket and wait my turn to be called.

The only ones who don't wait long are the ones who have it all.

Tapping my toe and waiting for class to dismiss.

Is this girl on T.V. going to hurry up give this guy a kiss?

Writing screenplays and novels, that I just can't do.

It takes too much time to get it where it's through.

I really don't want to talk too much on the telephone.

That's why I unplug it, and spend my time alone.

I really don't like to waste my precious time.

I won't waste yours either, I'll treat it just like mine.

What's my problem, do you to yourself say?

Time is too important to just dawdle it away.

Love and patience, they both go hand-in-hand.

It's not that I don't love you enough to wait, please do understand.

Time is a gift, too precious to throw away.

Make sure you've made time for your family today.

Vickie Vaughn Adams

Ship in A Bottle

An alcoholics bottle, resembles a bottomless cup.

An addicts needle is the place he prefers to sup.

Withered bodies, craving an empty high.

Go cold turkey? They'd rather lay down and die.

Love an addict, someone with a withered heart?

You give them all your love and they tear it all apart.

You model and show exactly what redemptive hearts should give.

All they do is take and take and seldom ever live.

A heart so tight, and tough a tasteless dried out fruit.

It has nothing to cling to, like a hollow rotten tooth.

You give and give yet they remain aloof.

Their wellspring is empty, so they just can't **hear** the truth.

Come out from your addiction, fight for your life.

Living in the ashcan of brokenness, is an open invitation to strife.

I have known many addicts, I try to speak from reason.

Addicts open ears , when it's their time and their season.

A prisoner of the fleeting, filled with tears of pain.

The prisoner wants out, it's truly driving him insane.

Come to me, you need me, is the deathly siren call.

Curled up with DT's - once *he had it all*!

Can't stop now, even if he tried.

He realizes now, that once he took those drugs with pride.

I want out, the prisoner, begs to be free.

Once upon a time, I drove you, now it's you who's driving me.

Heat

Hot rocks, wet feet

Dive into the cooling deep.

Sizzle and **pop**, like eggs on white hot road

Eighteen tires, **melt and buckle** under **hot** heavy loads.

Edges curl up on black pavement, white hot.

Aireate in a hammock, toss and turn on a cot.

Engines **smoke** from the churning **oiled** gears

Cowboys in heat chasing wild angry steers.

Sizzle from the heat of the **grill** and the pans.

Well **oiled** bodies sit and **fry** on the sand.

Restless task master cracks the whip,

Can't let up or productivity slips.

The drive for perfection, it never does cease.

Driven to be the best, so you persevere in the **heat**.

Never to stop or fail in the dirt,

A mouth full of **dust** – all bloodied and hurt.

Each day of your life, incessant heat drives you on,

Can't sleep or relax cause the heat is full on.

Sandy shores and limbs caressed by cool rippling waves.

A **cool** cup of water and much longed for shade.

THE SHELF

Books stand at attention on an old dusty shelf,

Awaiting fine citizens, thirsty for their wealth.

I was worried for a while that people no longer read.

Pages long silenced, falling open to fill empty heads.

At certain times in history, books were censored and burned.

Till indignity intervened and ceased what once was hated and spurned.

Freedom of speech relates to all written text,

If this freedom is snatched, who knows what comes next?

Substitution of media, electronic emulations.

Old grey matter *molting*, for lack of stimulation.

Bound up secrets from the bards of the past,

Books go the way of the dinosaur, they too did not last.

What would life be without those leaves bound in gold.

We'd still tend flocks and think that Earth was not so old.

No tales of exploration, seekers scaling the heights,

Scant information on Van Gogh and Dippers starry night.

Once in the past, slaves were forbidden to read.

In hatred beaten down and killed for educating their seed.

I'm ashamed that this bastion of knowledge is relegated to the past,

Do more than an occasional read, so volumes will continue to last.

I'm concerned that our culture has no true valuation,

for the utility of books in social education.

If the fruit of the nation, is literate apathy

In ten more years, where will our precious books be?

Funerary pyres piled miles high, reaching toward beaconing sky.

pearls of wisdom - ashes of knowledge must not surely die.

Strike a match, flicker of flame, incendiary desire

No books should perish on an irreverent funerary pyre.

Vickie Vaughn Adams

Glory!

Great and generous creator

Luminous, so darkness must flee

Orbiting this starlit galaxy

Resting His feet on stars and planets

Years to Him are as millennium

Beginners Haiku (5 -7 syllables)

Fa-	ther	a	li-	ght

Hel-	p	me	to	lo-	ve	you.

Now you try your hand at Haiku! (it's not easy!)

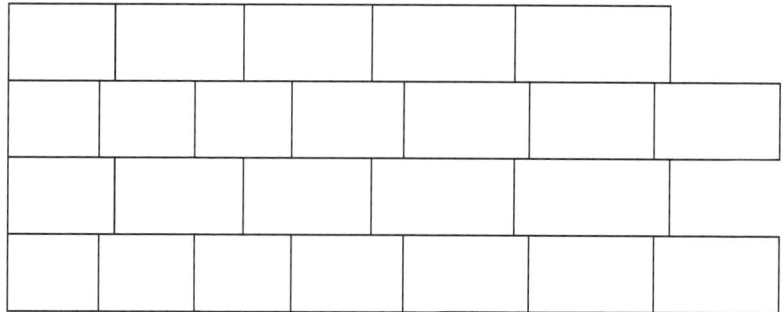

Pearls & Regret

You wish to enjoy what you sure have not earned,

You look back with longing, at the bridges *you've* burned.

Hard times falling like rocks on your head.

Reflecting back upon the cruel things you said.

Missed opportunity mixed with regret and then shame.

You have no one else, for your plight you can blame.

The best of my pearls I laid out for you.

Yours for the taking in full open view.

I never recall a more self serving swine-

You didn't choose me or our life serene and supine.

Make a choice, choose treasure or temporal respite.

Devoid of understanding, you just can't get it right!

I listen to your pleas for a moment of time,

You can recall now, what was yours is now mine.

Filled with regrets, you pound upon my securely shut door.

You now have no place in this heart anymore.

I served up my trust and topped it off with love.

You flung it away, like a distant star above.

Now, I ignore your pleas and you ponder aghast!

It was you who wanted things that would not last.

You stepped on me and ripped my open heart in two.

Now it's you who begs to me, and I abhor you!

I longed for a future with your sweetest embrace.

Now Karma flies back in your ungreatful face!

4 – FOLKS & STUFF
The Stalker

Multitudes of your solicitations, one every other day.

"*Oh valued one, I'll provide - if you please, <u>PLEASE</u> let me stay!*"

I miss you, I beg that **you** come back to me.

The only thing that I desire (*oh stalker*), is for you to let me be!

We had a bad confrontation, fifteen years in the past.

So, I was bound and determined that, **that** relationship would be our last.

My opinion is: I had "*good cause*" to sever all our ties.

You wanted things that were not yours, and bilked my trust with lies.

Family calls, to me they came from out the blue.

I needed more time to talk, what was I then to do?

I relented and asked you for your help again.

I though it worth the risk, for you to be my friend.

The heavy bond of our fellowship, I could no longer afford.

Closing the door on you, **again** - was of necessary accord.

Tiring of your harassment, to up the ante game.

I've tried to break it off, but you won't heed **my** refrain.

Finally, I get you to listen to me.

I think I've reached the finish line – now I feel home free!

A pathetic stalker, you begin the begging game.

What's your problem? Have you no ounce of shame?

The letters start again, it really bothers me.

That you my stalker have such *pomposity*!

Clearly you don't know, you've met your match in me.

You underestimate my personal desire to be free.

All you want is what's in my precious purse to give.

Have you no consideration, for what it costs to live?

I call for customer service, you put my calls on hold.

I used up all my cell minutes, this junk is getting old.

"*Cable, home phone service, DSL all great package deals.*

Compared to other service providers, our fees are quite a steal!"

I don't want the service, I'm trying to save something for me.

Why must you keep this hard-selling, these services **are not** free!

I call to cancel, you try to convince me that I'm wrong.

"Keep us a little longer to service your telephone."

I relent, because I tire of all the salesman talk,

I finally had to lie, to get you guys to walk.

How many times, and alternate ways must I say to you?

"Why pay for a monopoly, when I can circumvent these bills coming due?"

Cease and desist from your greedy selfish way!

Trying to gobble up all the customers, really doesn't pay.

You've turned me off to your wares, yet and still again.

Trying to force me into your court, will not make me a loyal friend.

Stop stalking me you evil cable provider.

Why pay when I can get service free, and have no bills from DSL-outsiders?

Wi-Fi RULES!!

Sincerely,

Buy, Buy telephone, and cable company (correction...)

Bye, Bye telephone and cable company

Carbs

Carbs are not the enemy of this I am convinced,

they're so tasty and delicious, how can it make sense?

The pastries, the cookies, cornbread and brimming muffin cups.

Can we have dinner without carbs, to complete our evening sup?

I've heard that sugar has been added, to the list of stimuli drugs.

The next thing you know Gingerbreadman will be labeled a useless thug!

My favorite tale is of Hansel & Gretel, breaking chunks from the witches house.

Something so delicious, can't be so bad when it's melting in your mouth.

Potatoes, oats, whole bran, legumes and semolina wheat.

Brown whole grain rice are all healthy carbs that you *can* eat.

Let us not rule out that buttery breads, pie and cake,

can also be enjoyed, without necessarily gaining weight.

The key is moderation in everything you do.

Just remember if you suck it down and not exercise – it'll stick to you like glue.

If I have no carbs, what really did I eat?

A plate full of grass – that leaves me feeling weak.

They say the USDA pyramid, was calculated wrong.

Lacking daily carbs, can we really grow up strong?

Frankly in my opinion and as far as I'm concerned –

with exercise and moderation, carbs can be efficiently burned.

Carbs aren't our enemy and we should end this fallatial thinking.

I see crisp freshly fried donuts, my ship has sailed and I am sinking!

Graduation Day

"Eat those veggies!" momma said, "That's why they're on your plate."

"Hurry Dear! Get up for school, this is the 2nd time you've been late."

"Pick your clothes up off the floor, make sure to get some rest."

"Grab your homework folder, we'll study for your test."

"Try not to run so fast, you might fall and cut your knee."

"Get down from that rickety treehouse, and let **that** furry critter free!"

"Sip this cod-liver oil and cherry vitamin supplement."

"Camping trip tomorrow, don't forget to pack your tent."

"Where is your yellow slicker and squeaky rubber boots?"

"Oh my! I have to show your friends the photo of **you** in your birthday suit!"

Graduation day, you're off to your new dorm.

"Always remember you'll need a raincoat to go out into a storm."

This time it's very different, momma won't be there.

She won't be able to help you pry the gum out of your hair.

You're all grown up now, you're off to a brand new life.

"I won't be there to brush away your tears and I'll try to limit my advice."

One day you'll understand what it means to love your child.

Trying to keep them safe from harm, with a loving smile.

Love and Kisses,

Momma

DEAR FRIEND

My Dearest Friend:

I know you're feeling down. That's why you sleep all day and can't get off the ground.

Lately things haven't gone as well as they should.

You tried so hard and did the very best you could.

Your last relationship didn't turn out so well.

At that recent interview, yourself you couldn't sell.

It's hard to keep moving, on those cloudy days.

But the winners don't give up, it's what the people say.

You've kept close to me your single and best-est friend.

You've no one else to share hopes and fears with, or the victories that you win.

Things will improve, continue hanging on.

It's time to lift the veil of doubt and hear birds beauteous song.

Feel free to give yourself a well-deserved mental break.

Winners know that failure is a chance to learn from their mistake.

Remember that your closest and best friend is you.

There's no one else who's as clever and great at what they do.

Life escalates, with experiences up and down.

Just as you're about to throw it in, things can turn completely around.

We're not all to be Hollywood glamorous or famous movie stars.

We are what we were meant to be, and that's just who **you** are.

I'm so proud to know you and have you as my friend.

Now, get up and enjoy life – let's not have this talk again!

Smile friend, tomorrow is a new day!

Tough Times

A once booming U.S. economy, years past hit the skids.

It all boils down to greedy people, the fallout and what they hid.

Fiscal principals built on usury, abhorrent and despised.

The **abomination** of oppressive kingdoms, face Babylonian demise.

Megalomaniacs, hoarding the power and the loot,

desirous of power, symptomatic of rotten root.

The USA **Titanic** hit a rock, never thought that we would sink.

The greed of **megabanks** has pulled us all toward a disasterous, abysmal **brink**.

Spiritual **wickedness** in high and low places.

Misery piled up in corners, prayers screamed up into heavenly spaces.

Desperately searching for gainful **employment** – a quest going on for years.

Can't afford food any more, inert and sieged by fears.

Banks go belly up, families vacate homes.

Millions in **default**, because they relied on **subprime loans**.

A *7th Year of Jubilee*, was a custom of the ancient Jew.

It gave the in**debt**ed a chance to recover and start life fresh and new.

A dead-end **economy**, where only two classes prevail

The extremely rich and desperately poor, the **middle class** has failed.

Alliances collapsing, reliance on Chinese wealth.

At one point we were able, now no longer can we help ourself.

Extremely **ungreatful** for the blessings that we've had

Now, they've disappeared and life has gone extremely bad.

One way out, it's not one we can see,

 it involves knees hitting floor and crying out to Thee.

Lord help us, to return from the bowels of self-destruction.

Cease our sinning ways and banish media seduction.

The feelings that parents have for a child, God has same and surely chides.

Only He can bridge the brink and rescue man from a plummet into a great divide.

In Memoriam

I knew a girl, who came from a dysfunctional home.

Her name was Octavia, she always felt alone.

She had a sister, but they were not the closest of friends.

Octavia, was somehow isolated even up until the end.

Her mom was a raging alcoholic addicted to the brew.

As the two sisters grew up, this is all the life they knew.

Sometimes there was no food and strangers in and out the house.

"*Sit down and shut up!*" said their mother, or "*I'll slap your silly mouth*!"

I heard Octavia had passed today, she went to the hospital by herself.

Something went wrong and she cried out to the nurse , "*Please Help*!"

She wailed in pain and gave up her ghost with a shattering scream.

That was the end of Octavia and all her hopes and dreams.

Octavia had four kids, they were separated like valued stock.

Some had dads who cared and others had dads with hearts of rock.

I had hated to be at her funeral that sad and downcast day, as they

parted the children from their mothers grave and sent them all a separate way.

What bothered me most when Octavia died that day,

She had no loved one there, to see her on her way.

Had her boyfriend taken time to stay and hold her hand,

She might have gotten help and not met such a pitiable painful end.

I saw how she searched for love, in the ruins of her life.

She allowed herself to be abused and she struggled with inward strife.

She had the temper of a tiny evil imp,

but she worked like a soldier and never made a wimp.

She'd saved her money and took care of all her bills,

but I understand that after the funeral, they rushed to read her will.

The boyfriend she lived with before she passed away,

had planned to take her house, after disposing of her stuff post-funeral day.

He wasted no time, getting himself another girl.

I'll always remember Octavia, because she was a damaged pearl.

Rest in peace my friend, I remember you even now.

I'm sorry that I wasn't there to help you through that fateful day somehow.

I remember your cute, little brown-eyed kids.

I know they won't forget the hard work, for them that **you** did.

No one should ever leave this world feeling abandoned and alone.

I know you are at peace in your heavenly home.

You climbed up on the rough side of this mountain called life,

Now the trek is over and it's the end of your strife.

The Prize Fight!

At night laying on my bed and watching the small T.V.

A bug jumped on my head and boy you should've seen me!

I shot up like bullet and dropped some things on the floor.

I couldn't rest until that bug wasn't there anymore.

Was it a roach or a spider, perhaps a stinging bee?

Not sure what it was, but I wanted if off of me!

I had no roaches in the apartment where I lay.

So, that was out, I'll search for that vicious bug until the break of day.

I threw up the sheets and turned on the light.

That bug wasn't getting out of here free tonight!

The balcony door is often open, when I try to get fresh air,

But the drawback is that bugs fly in, when I'm seated there.

Well, on with the story and my quest for vindication.

Vickie Vaughn Adams

That darn bug will regret causing me this aggravation!

The covers were off and I flung them away from the bed,

I had to see what it was creeping upon my head.

I saw it, I saw it, I caught a fleeting glimpse,

but it limped out of my sight and moved quick, like an imp!

It kept trying to crawl back under the shelter of my bed.

Can't give up now, I'd rather abandon my rest instead.

I kicked the fitted sheet and pushed the pillow askew.

I spotted him again as he crept away, a blue-blackish hue.

I stomped upon his back, with my squishy flowered flip-flop.

The pressure wasn't enough to make this bad bug stop!

I'm in a darkened room – I knocked my lamp over,

I could have given this bug a leash and named him Range-Rover.

I could see sufficiently to continue my prize winning fight,

couldn't sleep at all, if this bug took a second flight.

I got him, I got him – I finally stunned that pest!

I was so happy, he wouldn't go home tonight to his comforting nest.

It was crawling towards the window, seeking an escape.

He shouldn't have lept on me, 'cause now it's just too late.

What's The Deal?

In my opinion it seems respect has gone out of style.

In order to find it, you have to walk a country mile.

Bullies, foul mouths are rampant on the tube.

Bodies exposed, broadcast murders, raucous and extremely crude.

Cyber-fights are recorded using cellphones on the sly.

Media violence and murder are at an all time high.

Some cities hold the title of Murder Capital U.S.A.

Yet, the cops are being laid-off in cities everyday.

Budget cuts, city managers slashing services for the poor.

But politicians and bankers are taking money out our back door.

Missing children on posters, eyes with vacant stares.

This stuff has been happening since the 70's, does anyone still care?

Moma's kill their children, due to their unrest.

A crime, that can't be logically explained *nor* openly confessed.

I saw a homeless couple begging from strangers driving by,

Avoid eye contact, is it needed or just a bold-faced lie?

Mental illness, of exponentially varied and evolving types.

Conspicuous consumption of drugs they smoke inside their pipes.

Each decade has its challenges, the degradation of life and respect.

Weirdoes getting famous and even now their tiny pets.

In my opinion respect should never go out of style.

Not in the urban jungle or the walk of a country mile.

It gets kind of tedious, preaching to people who don't listen.

Respect won't return to our land, as long as we think gold is **all** that glistens.

Desk Serenade

Desks in the class go round and round.

Bobby Morgan, will you please sit down.

Please be quiet for the second time.

Bobby Morgan take your place in the back of the line.

Jenny did you finish this assignment today?

It's time for recess, now run over and play!

It's your turn to lead the pledge.

Get yourself down off that window ledge.

Darian Jones you're disturbing class again today,

Wait until lunch and share what you have to say.

Darian, I'd appreciate you turning around.

Stop making faces like a circus clown.

Wash those hands before you eat your lunch.

You'll go see the principal, if you throw that punch!

Peel the Elmer's glue off your hands.

Cease banging on the desk, you are not in band!

Open your text to page one hundred four.

Stop being silly and waving out the door.

Collect your papers and clear the floor.

You can't eat that candy, and act hyper any more.

Teaching is filled with tons of verbs.

Because the classroom etiquette must be observed.

The most delightful thing of all,

Is to see each and every student in the fall.

Word Play

flashflood =	Water and lightening, *hmmmm*?
wetwork =	Extremely uncomfortable employment conditions?
dumbfound =	Do you actually think a dumb person would be successful finding anything?
killjoy =	Murder madness, Joy won't do too well.
gifthorse =	Try getting this thing into a box.
firestorm =	Wouldn't the storm put out the flames?
quicksand =	It takes a while to get this sand out of your shorts.

peacepipe	=	Not so peaceful in a nonsmoking room.
headhunter	=	You'd better duck and _stay_ down!
stormchaser	=	Talking about a bad career decision! Watch out for the "_blowhards._"
rollback	=	Water off a duck.
Pleasant Valley	=	Everything rolls down hill !

Now you add two:

=	

REMEMBRANCE

The bible says, "*All is vanity*". In everything we do,

None of this matters if it's just about me and you.

We run and stay busy all day, is this expenditure a dividend's deal?

We all wear out, inert investments - we're not made of steel.

Clean the house, make the food again.

It's a never ceasing cycle that will eventually end.

Our bodies get weak and eyes grow dim.

Have we invested enough time in Him?

Time earning money and chasing our special cause.

Do we meditate and take time to pause?

It's the heart and soul that survives this life-

The faith in God to help relieve this strife.

An investment in things eternal do pay,

Lord I'm so glad you're here with me today.

I've encountered trials and my body's in pain.

Please forgive me if I have complained.

Thank you for taking care of my family.

For establishing my cause and taking up the fight for me.

I'm so glad that I have food and a good warm bed.

I can have peace when I lay down my head.

As I went about to do my work,

You made sure that I was not hurt.

It's great to have a friend as close as Thee.

Thank you for caring eternally for me.

The hidden danger that I failed to see,

You sent angels in front to take care of me.

Praise is all I have to offer You, that really might matter much.

Thanks is a sweetened savor that's keeps heaven at our touch.

Agua

I do love my water so crystal clean and clear.

I ask the waitress, "*Do you sell the bottled here?*"

She says "**No**", so I push away the glass.

There are some bad diseases, that dirty water can pass.

Water springs up from the ground deep within its bowels.

When you shower, pollutants and contaminants will remain upon the towels.

I strive not to drink the city water from the tap.

I saw what came out when the maintenance man cleaned my faucet trap.

I don't use tap water for cooking food and meat.

If water's floridated, it's supposed to help your teeth.

Research says that fluoride and chlorine, aren't that good for you.

They're both carcinogens that make a cancerous brew.

Vickie Vaughn Adams

I love coffee and even red Kool-Aid.

But I'm particular about the water from which they both are made.

My water comes in a jug an extra filtrated drink.

When growing up, I had water that was brown and had a stink.

They say there was no problem with Edward's water at all,

But when Grandma would say," *Drink it*!", I would try to stall.

For whatever reason, I'm particular about my glass.

It's got to do with the pollution in the environment and how long it will last.

I can't drink this water, if I think it isn't clean.

It's due to caution and tastebuds and not because I'm mean.

Factory pollutants run into ponds and lakes,

While EPA is sleeping, we'll have to live with the choices **they** make.

You know who you are dumping that garbage into our freshwater source. We live in a 70% world. The Earth, our bodies, plant life (all living organisms) are seventy + percent water. With all of the water on Earth, only a percentage is fresh and potable.

My Favorite Chore

I hate hauling stinky laundry up and down the stairs.

I'd rather push a lawnmower and pick green grass out my hair.

Pushing the vacuum up and down brown carpet shag.

Then fighting off the dust-bunnies escaping from the bag.

Washing windows is hard, trying to get all of the streaks,

Cleaning out the bird cage - as it pecks me with its beak.

The chore I really, really, really don't like the most,

Is cleaning up the burnt crumbs after making breakfast toast.

Pull out the fridge drawer and wipe out brown lettuce leaves.

Make sure crushed tomatoes haven't left any tiny seeds.

Move the shower curtains, getting smudges off the wall.

Running out of spray cleaner to glisten the shower stall.

Next to last detail, dusting tiny end tables.

The long one with the computer, is not very good and stable.

Now we move on outside, I'm sweeping off the deck.

Did I get the charcoal stains? I'd better double-check.

I'm nearly done right now, climbing up to the attic.

There's so much fiber insulation, my hair is pulled by static.

Of all the chores and work I do within the house, the worst

chore I can think of, is cleaning up a tiny dead mouse!

Tiny Mickey Jr. got caught by his little tail.

I have to grab my heavy yellow gloves to get him in the pail.

This job takes extra equipment, gloves, mask and broom.

I sweep him up, disinfect and get this critter out of the room!

I'll take all the extra chores piled one on top of another.

If I don't have to carry another Mickey out along with his friends and brothers.

 ## DREAMERS

Children are born with a dream and song is their tiny heart.

It's up to parents to help them get a phenomenal start.

Curiosity if nurtured can ignite magnificent sparks.

Without the love of a parent the rainbow will not arc.

Those who are tended with love and generous care,

Climb heights unimagined that adults will not dare.

I've seen so many lights extinguished at birth.

Tiny souls washed away never to touch this old Earth.

Songs never sung and waltzes not danced.

Genius uncultivated, never stood a chance.

As a child we can remember having such lofty dreams.

I want to play piano, compose a song then sing!

Push aside the cocoon and bring forth my art,

Dance on a stage and really play my part.

In your care you have such gifts, take care that

their spirits aren't broken and their voices they can lift.

God gave you children, each one can make you proud,

You must open your eyes and sing their praises loud.

"My child you did well. What more can I say?"

"I'm truly honored to be your parent today!"

Even if they fail or things don't go just right.

Make sure that they know, it's okay to err before you kiss them goodnight.

"You gave your very best, when you played out on the field."

For their little accomplishments, make them a big deal.

Too often children are crushed in the womb.

They hobble through life burdened, dead and entombed.

They had no voice and definitely no say,

As to whether or not they wanted to come this way.

I encourage you parents to just take a chance.

Help your child succeed and teach them to dance.

You'll be so proud and so glad that you did,

light this candle for the world, and it's radiance was not hid.

Vickie Vaughn Adams

Advice for Bullies

Each human child is born with a sense of fair play. We all know what is, and is not the righteous way.

So you like to bully others, shooting off your dirty mouth. You don't like it when someone is tearing down your house.

If it's not edification coming from your face, you need to revisit your priorities, cause you've become a real disgrace.

Bully are you puffed up and proud of yourself? I think you need to ask someone for serious help.

Targeting smaller people makes you feel real strong. When deep down inside you know it's all wrong!

No one in our sphere should be suffering with shame, home is a place that no one should be in pain.

Slaps across the face, struck with brooms and bats, the blows to self esteem are so much worse than that.

Cause mom, pop, brother or sis crushed your poor heart down, doesn't give you the liberty to push other people around.

I'm sorry that the life you have, some how seems to stink, but sometimes bullies need a wakeup call to stop and think.

There's been war and rivalry since Cain his brother killed. But repentance and forgiveness has been Gods ultimate will.

What makes people's legacy a replay of traumas past? Perpetuate hate towards a brother and the same betrayal lasts.

I know you should understand how other people feel, when they've endured the wrath of your vicious upturned heel.

Would you wish on someone else the deep agony perpetrated on you? – you need to find some help to get you through!

When you do those mean things, is your anger ever quenched? Or does it rise yet again and rage until it's spent?

If someone's hurting you, seek help, share the pain. I've walked where you have and felt the same.

Stop this madness, change your behavior, that's what you can do. Be a better person that that bully was to you.

Communicate with your victim, try to be a friend. You may find it rewarding to support and not offend.

Be for someone else what you would like to have. This very act could soothe your soul and act just like a healing salve.

There's no better feeling than modeling what you need. Being a good example is planting worthy seed.

5 – SCIENCE RIPS

Look At Those Genes!

Thomas M. Hunt studied flies to learn of chromosomes. Lots of flies and ripened fruit, I'm sure he spent tons of time alone.

Fruit flies are small and very easy to feed. Hunt used them to study, because they very quickly breed.

The flies had large chromosomes and rapidly reproduced. Hunt studied them for fly-eye color and wing shape, I'm telling you the truth!

In 1952 the molecule DNA was identified. Rosalind Franklin photographed exactly what she spied.

The photos showed that DNA was twisted like a spiral stair.

Her pictures proved it really actually was there.

Rosalind Franklin was a very smart Brit,

she helped prove that DNA was scientifically legit!

Next we have Mr. Watson and Mr. Crick.

They continued the study of DNA using Rosalind's pics.

They used her work to build a model to show,

that DNA has two long strands, connected by shorter strands—did **you** know?

Watson and Crick received a Nobel Prize in 1962,

but they used the work of others to make models of something not so new.

So in summary, we have learned so much you see, of what a scientific method and inquiry can and should be!

 ## Perfect Combinations

I'm a savy scientist and I'm here today, to explain solutions and mixtures in a simple way.

A mixture is formed when two or more substances are combined.

There can be very large pieces *or* some extremely fine.

Although they are tossed together they remain what they are.

If you can find the big or small bits – you're really a spelunking star.

A fruit salad or maybe sand and stone.

You can sort, pick-apart and separate the pieces and put them all alone.

The key thing is that a mixture can be picked apart,

because the atoms are separated, not melded together from the start.

However, with a compound it's really not the same.

The atoms are combined together , an example is acid rain.

A compound becomes something totally new.

Different from a mixture, but they both contain *at least two*.

Are you a combination or compound of mom and dad?

Compare the two descriptions and decide if being a mixture is good or bad!

The Producers

Producers sit at the base of the food chain.

The life of producers depend on gasses, sun and rain.

Producers are organism that make food from light.

They can't hunt, travel or make food at night.

People need oxygen, producers carbon **di-ox-ide**.

We need them, they need us, this is how we both survive.

When we exchange our gasses both species win,

without the oxygen from producers—people would meet a painful end.

Organisms in the oceans carry out photosynthesis too.

Producers use their adaptations like chlorophyll and leaves to make themselves some food.

Organisms called consumers don't make their own food.

They eat other plants and animals, don't you find this crude?

Herbivores, omnivores and carnivores make three.

Two of them are meat-eaters and one can eat from a tree.

The Kikajous can eat small animals, insects or plants.

This can come in handy if proteins are very scant.

Remember that producers make their own food.

We should really value them, save trees and plankton— be thankful don't be crude.

PEACE IN THE MIDDLE EAST & AMERICA

ABOUT THE AUTHOR

The author Vickie Vaughn Adams, is a native of Vicksburg, Mississippi. She also spent much of her youth in Louisiana. She is a former USAF military veteran, who obtained her B.A. Degree at the University of Michigan-Flint. She is currently pursuing her Masters in Special Education. She has published two other books: "The Misadventures of Sticky & Leo". A tale chronicling the actions of a disabled boy and his mate. The second vanity publication is the "Women & Girl's Survival Guide: Everything You Want to Know, But No One Would Tell You. The guide is a self-help book that stresses personal and social safety issues. She is the founder of V&V Educational GAMES. This company develops, produces and markets educational materials for families or institutions. She has two children and several grandchildren. She currently resides in the State of Michigan.

Made in the USA
Charleston, SC
21 July 2011